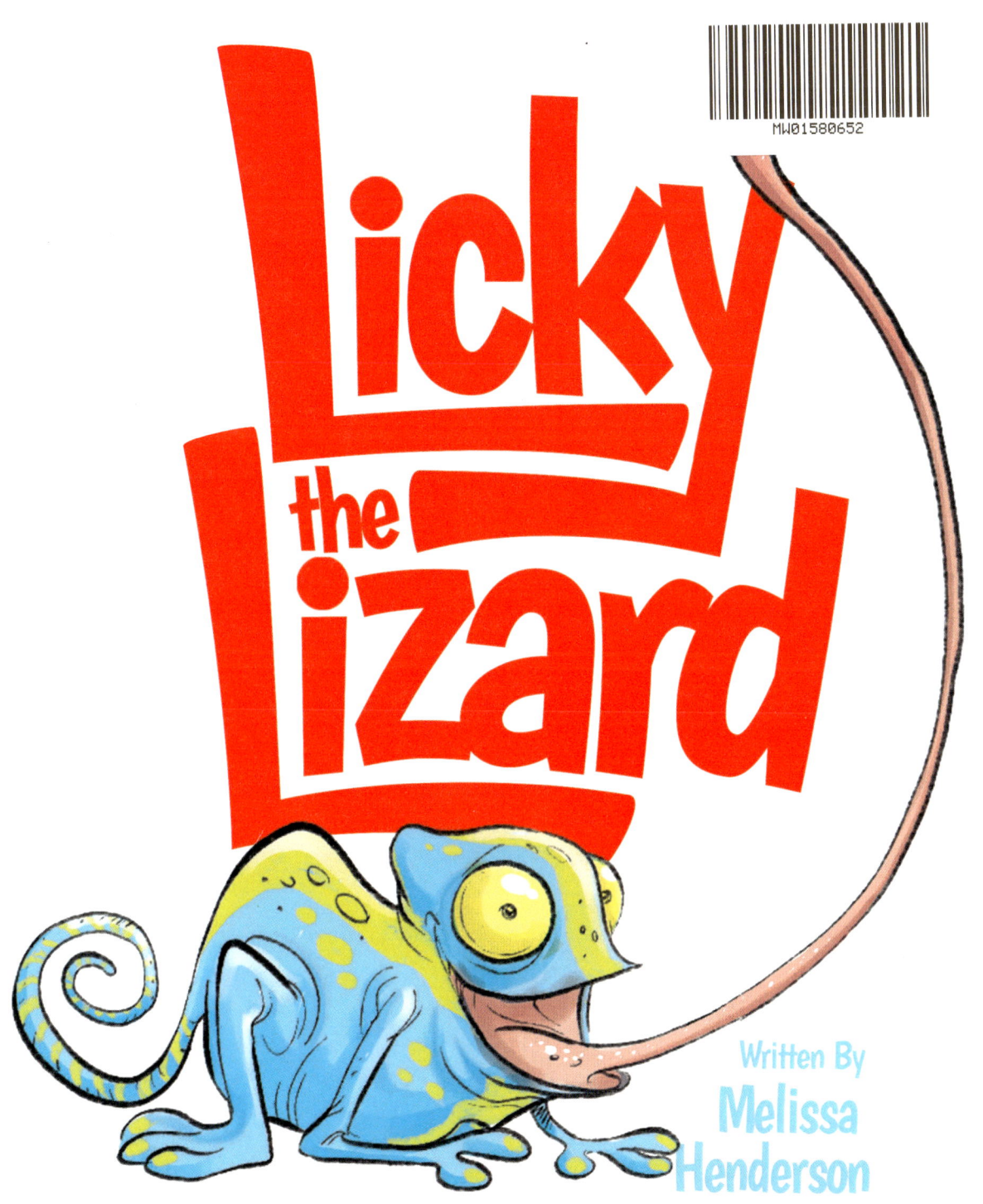

Palmetto Publishing Group
Charleston, SC

Licky the Lizard
Copyright ©2018 Melissa Henderson
Illustrations by Mark Brayer

All rights reserved. No part of this publication may be reproduced, distributed, stored in a retrieval system, or transmitted, in any form or by any means, including electronic, mechanical, photocopying, recording or otherwise, without the prior written permission of the publisher, except in the case of brief quotations embodied in critical reviews, and certain other non-commercial uses permitted by copyright law.

First Edition

Printed in the United States

ISBN-13: 978-1-64111-139-3
ISBN-10: 1-64111-139-9

This book is dedicated to Mike.

Thank you for being the most encouraging, inspiring and patient son.

Dad and I are very proud of you.

My name is Licky Lizard.

Friends call me Licky because I like to stick out my tongue and catch things that are floating in the air.

Today, I was enjoying the bright sunshine on the brick wall next to the front door of a house.

I closed my eyes and went to sleep.

Ahhh . . . warm sunshine and a nap.

All at once, a loud voice woke me.

"Yikes! A lizard!"

A lady stood there, looking at me with big eyes.

She was afraid of me.

She was shaking.

Her hair was standing straight up in the air.

I started shaking. I was afraid of her.

"Yikes! A lady!" I thought to myself.

I wanted the lady to know that lizards are friendly.

God created lizards, and God created the lady, too.

She didn't have to be afraid of me.

We kept staring at each other,

both of us with our big eyes.

Finally, she looked closer at me and stopped shaking.

Her hair calmed down.

I looked at her and stopped shaking.

"Hello, little lizard. I am sorry if I frightened you.

You surprised me!"

She had surprised me, too.

We stared at each other for awhile longer.

Enjoying the sunshine together would be fun.

Now, every time the friendly lady goes in and out of her house, she calls to me and says, "Hello, lizard friend!"

I say hello back to the lady by sticking out my tongue.

Remember, we are all God's creations. He loves us all.

ABOUT THE AUTHOR

Melissa Henderson and her husband Alan live in coastal South Carolina. She continues to write Christian stories, and also enjoys writing for her blog. Her passions include volunteering in church and in the community, Bible studies, reading and writing, and sharing special moments with family.

Made in the USA
Middletown, DE
21 May 2019